In the name of Allah, the most beneficent, the most merciful

Even to myself I was so wrong the first time
When a stone in hand I stood along the first time

Silence that Echoed

Khwaja Wahab Sabir

Translation by Mudassir A. Khan
from Sadaye Sukhan

First Paperback Edition:	September 2020
Book Name:	Silence that Echoed
	(Translated from Sadaye Sukhan)
Category:	Poetry
Language:	English
Poet:	Khwaja Wahab Sabir
	khwajawahab@sbcglobal.net
	P.O.Box 9298
	Vallejo, CA 94591, USA
Translation:	Mudassir A. Khan
Title Cover:	Raja Ishaq
Publisher:	Andaaz Publications
	4616 E Jaeger Rd
	Phoenix, AZ 85050 USA
Email:	admin@andaazpublications.com
Ordering Information:	Available from amazon.com and
	other retail outlets

To Nafisa Wahab
and
Umma Amina

Breaking of heart is what gain to you
What will this act seek in vain to you

Contents

Preface

A desire to learn and live a better life gravitated me to the United States of America. I packed my bag for Chicago in 1978. It was unlike when I, with my parents, crossed the border during the bloodbath of the partition of India from Hyderabad Deccan to Pakistan. In no way my moving to the USA could be compared to the great migration in the Islamic History when Prophet Muhammad (PBUH) left Mecca to Medina with his followers. I merely changed my country for a better life.

Belonging to a literary family, the love for Urdu literature permeated in my heart. While the lap of my mother kept revealing the life upon me, my grandmother gently massaged my sensitivity to feel the pain of others.

She was a poetess with a pen name of Aajiza. She kept composing poems, not knowing her beautiful words were touching my heart in her lap.

As she grew older, grandmother lost her eyesight. Her pen stopped, but her brain kept composing beautiful poetry. I chose to reveal her words on the piece of paper. She spoke out loud, and I poured ink on her enlightening words. Each poem of her elevated me to the next level. By the time she left the world, the seed of a poet had sprouted in me.

I stepped into the vast desert of the Urdu Poetry and found refuge in its soft sand from the sharp spines of the oasis of the world.

I pray for my elders' departed souls for turning me into a humble human being and enlivening the poetic sensibility upon me. With that, I hope that you will get something positive out of my Urdu Poetry translation in English.

Stay blessed.

Khwaja Wahab Sabir

A Bond Between Culture and Tradition

I mmersed in his quietude, I saw Sabir in one of the Urdu Academy North America's programs in the bay area. That was our first acquaintance that soon turned into a friendship. As a humble and down to earth person, he never spoke of his poetry, unlike many others. I am pleasantly surprised to see the manuscript of his poetry, which came to me through my friend Fayyaz Uddin Saieb.

Tradition and culture are intertwined in Sabir's poetry with the simple way of expression. While I see many young poets going against the tide of tradition to bring a fresh perspective, I found Sabir carrying its shades with a modern touch.

It appears that his poetic sensitivity draws a wide variety of topics. The moment a thought touches his heart, he picks up the pen and infuses his emotions into words.

Human desires touch our hearts in different ways. What may seem a matter of shoulder-shrugging for many, draws Sabir to dissect it to reach what lies at the core level that triggers the aspiration.

Love and friendship keep the spark smoldering in our lives. In the materialistic society we live in, the altruism seemed to be lacking in human interactions. Sabir didn't let this feeling go unnoticed and emphatically touches it in his various poems, yet a different style.

I hope that Sabir continues to write and wish him all the best!

Tashie Zaheer
Urdu Academy North America

Reflection of the Fragrance

T hose who could let the fragrance on the crest of air
Are with Urdu elegance on the crest of air

As poet said above, I had a similar feeling while reading Sabir's poetic work, Silence that Echoed. While various names come to our mind who have paved a new path in Urdu Poetry with their unique style, Parveen Shakir stands prominent with her vivid imagination of reflection of the fragrance.

Her poetic diction reached to the people throughout the world where Urdu Poetry touches hearts. She encouraged many novices like me to follow her on this journey.

Reading Sabir's poetry, I felt the same touch that once had inspired me, and it took me to the process of transference. Yet, it was his poetry that held my hand, and I walked along, experiencing the journey. I smelled the aroma of many flowers, saw their vivid colors, and touch their soft petals. Sabir said:

> Today weather whispered of your arrival
> Is it the breeze or a present smell of yours

I applaud Sabir for taking me on such an incredible poetic journey where I not only waived my hands to Parveen Shakir but also saw a glimpse of Khumar Barabankvi and Amjad Islam Amjad.

I wish he continues to blend the ink of his pen with emotions and carve the words which would on the fragrance wings reach to the poetry lovers without any boundaries,

Dr. Habib Khan
Arizona

Translator's Preface

I was not familiar with Sabir's work before seeing his Urdu Poetry book Sadaye Sukhan. So, I read his work with curiosity to understand the poet. His voice in his verses talked to me, and the more I read, the more I was impressed.

In his work, I found depth, philosophy, mysticism, love, pain, cute wordplay, tough refrains being used with ease. He celebrated the successes and the good in the people, references to historical events about his personal experiences, but then also his empathy and suffering of others.

I consider Sabir, a poet of love and celebrations. He celebrates life in general, but his central theme essentially is love. This love is down to earth with his awe and adoration for beauty and nature. He talks about the pretty woman and her teases. He refers to her teases that he, on its receiving end, disguises as hardships but enjoys the pangs deep inside of himself. Sabir regards these pains as gifts bestowed by his beloved. His intensity of love in his poems reminded me of E.E. Cummings. Now, his love and the nature surrounding it do not just end with that passion because then Sabir takes another step and declares that his everlasting love is with his pen and his writing. It also keeps him going to keep writing about love, nature, and humanity.

Sabir takes life seriously and encourages the reality of the problems that can arise continuously. He points out that we should remind ourselves of the overlooked things in life and advises us of humility and gratefulness. Sabir tells us that death is around the corner and that no one is going to go on their own terms when the time comes. The way he, in his own way, describes this matter would make Emily Dickinson proud (reference poem: Because I could not stop for Death by Emily Dickinson). Below are a few translated couplets from one of Sabir's ghazals (a type of a poem explained elsewhere in this book):

Matters do not cease and keep coming in arrays
Problems do keep on increasing in all their ways

I have been carrying love affair with my pen
It is affairs like these that are my getaways

There is well being in walking with a head bowed
It just takes a moment for life to end and faze

No one merrily dresses and lies in coffin,
When the time to go comes Sabir, no one then stays.

Besides beauty and nature, Sabir also appreciates art in whatever form it is created in and admirers the artists. He applauds the sculptors but then reminds them that while they take soil from the earth and make faces and bodies out of them, God also has fashioned humans' life from clay. Then with an amusing tactfulness, he adds that God can even breathe life into the sculptures that he has created, but the ordinary sculptor cannot achieve this feat.

Throughout his work, Sabir has references to melodies. He talks about the melodious enchanting voice of the beloved. Sabir goes into lengths about how the sounds and motions of dances affect him. But then he is also appreciative of others. Showing admiration of singing as art, he pays homage with an ode to "Diana Krall," the famous singer and jazz pianist. He beautifully crafts a poem in (continuous) ghazal form showering admiration according to him about the genius of her artistic talents.

He rises to the occasion to console people that have suffered disasters such as earthquakes. He refers to the different dreams of people that are harshly interrupted within a moment. The calamity of an earthquake stops the people of different ages thinking in their respective dreams and senses with the young ones of future hopes and dreams, while the elderly with their daydreaming reminiscing their good old memories and reliving those in their minds. Suddenly it is all stopped. Even the cattle, with the jingling musical bells, is interrupted with nonmusical sounds.

Sabir, like many poets, has deep feelings for people that are harmed and oppressed. He is shocked at the Peshawar incident when someone carried a bombed towards a school and was stopped by a fellow student at the gate, and the bomb exploded, killing many students nearby. In his poem "A Mother's Woe on Peshawar Tragedy," he writes it in the point of view of a mother of one of those children that died in the incident. He laments that the boy was there at the house a few moments ago full of life before he left for school, and then very soon after that, he was brought lifeless into her arms. The mother is beside herself and questions the loyalties of people that commit such inhuman atrocities.

Sabir also is a champion of people's self-determinations. In a poem, he addresses the "People of Kashmir" and expresses that they will be united with their loved ones and that they will be free.

Above, I have mentioned just a few samples from his work. Sabir is an excellent multi-generation poet. He possesses the soul of a poet. He addresses topics from mysticism and philosophies of life to love with the beloved and then all the down to earth facts of life with their celebrations of happiness as well as the sadness of tragedies.

In the chapter Translator's Thoughts on Translating Urdu Poetry, I will define the styles of the theme of Urdu poetry used by Sabir in his work as well as the issues that have surrounded us, poetry translators, when translating poetry into another language.

Mudassir A. Khan

Thoughts on Translating Urdu Poetry

This chapter is derived and has direct quotes from the preface of my work of Ghalib's translations and my other works. Here I will go over some of the themes used in Urdu poetry as well as my theory on translating Urdu poetry.

I regard the translating of poetry as a completely separate art and craft within the broader bounds of poetry. Translating a poem from one language into another is like migrating from one culture onto another. Though the essential words in the respective languages serve the same meanings in the dictionaries when the words join other words and create local idioms, then they create their own subcultures around their topics. It leads to local references to customs and provides the poet with some great opportunities for puns and wordplay.

Poets use vast vocabulary and enjoy wordplay when they write their poems. So, some idiom used in one language means whatever it is supposed to mean along with the poet's pun added upon it. Still, when it is translated into another language, it can completely lose its appeal and, at times, sound odd due to it not making sense.

Sometimes I use a corresponding idiom or a reference in the translated language. For example, there is a common theme of using "Toor" or "Mountain of Toor" in Arabic, Persian, Turkish, and Urdu and some other related languages and poetries. Toor in these languages is the name of the mountain on which Moses went to meet his God. We know of the story of the burning bush. It is the same incident. But when I translate the references to that story, I do not use the word Toor or Mount Toor; instead, I use the English term for it, which is Mount Sinai.

So, at times it is better to use the local language's word or terms when translating a poet. On the other hand, at times, I leave alone the theme or words indigenous to the original language of the poems and do not use the prevalent local terms of the language the poems are translated into. For example, when it comes to "Laila and Majnun," a famous love story from the Middle East, I keep it as is and use Laila and Majnun as their names and references to their own life events. I do not use Juliet for Laila and Romeo for Majnun. As we know, Romeo and Juliet is a famous love story in the English language.

So, now going back to my saying that translating from one language or culture is like migrating. When people migrate or even when they move within the same culture, they must pack up things, then after the move unpack and then rearrange their stuff at the new place.

As a kid, I was used to traveling due to my father's work as a diplomat. At a young age, I had learned that when one moves, some things get lost while some items get broken. Furthermore, I also realized that at the new place, the things and the furniture do not get placed the same way as it was at the previous location. This usually was due to different architectures and layouts of the houses. Then the building codes may vary.

Similarly, when translating a poem, I come across things that may fit well in the original language would not be as appealing to the translated language. Furthermore, when in structured poems such as ghazal, a whole new set of challenges arises. In a ghazal, there can be a refrain, which is a repeated word or a phrase at the end of a verse or the second line of a couplet.

Now, when translating from Urdu into English or vice versa is a considerable challenge since the subject and object in language structures are in reverse order between English and Urdu. In English, the subject comes first, and then the object comes after (the verb). In Urdu, on the other hand, the object comes first and then the subject.

The reverse nature of the subject and order between English and Urdu brings about the challenge of repeating the refrains at the end of the verse lines where they show up. This is tough because the refrain must maintain its meaning and the tense it is being used in. The reverse order of the subject and object can completely change the meanings at times. So, in translated work, the refrain not only has to be translated accurately but has to be carried at the end of the line(s).

Now, I want to go over what the poem form ghazal is. It is the most famous poetry form in Urdu. It is a poem that has a series of couplets (two-liners) that have rhymed endings of the second line. Each couplet is independent in meaning, and it is like mini poems of two lines lined up in series bound by rhyme or refrain with rhyme. The sound effect of the different meanings but with rhymed endings is mesmerizing for the listener or the reader.

The themes in ghazals vary from love to everyday life. People write about oppression, injustice, wooing of beloved, economic hardships, etc. There is no rule on the topics. The requirement is that it should rhyme at the end. In the traditional ghazal languages, a strict established metered form must be maintained. In English ghazals, the meter is not enforced, but it is recommended that whatever is the number of syllables of the first line should be maintained in all the lines of that ghazal. Hence, if the first line of a ghazal has 14 syllables, then all the lines of the ghazal have to have the same number of syllables.

The ghazals are untitled. In the first couplet, both the lines are rhymed. Then only the second lines of each couplet are rhymed. The second lines maintain rhymed words, and at times a fixed refrain follows the rhymes. Here, I want to point out that in published works, when the ghazals are listed in the list of contents, the first line or the refrain can be listed with the page number that he ghazal is located on. This is only a nominal reference for the readers to find certain ghazals. This still does not mean that the ghazal has been provided a title. The ghazals, by their nature, have to be untitled. This adds to the magnificent grandiosity of the ghazal form of poetry.

Mudassir A. Khan

I t's my existence's only pursue O God
That when I worship, it is only you O God

Wherever I happen to look, I see your sights
Aromatic you 're in each venue O God

Grateful, I whisper your name on each prayer bead
May humbly be enlightened my value O God

What may seem present besides you is mortal here
Blood affirms that when it runs in veins through O God

This is the only humble prayer of Sabir
Everywhere your kindness to continue O God

One day master will invite me in Medina
This is my hope that I will be in Medina

It will be your favor to my eyes, O master
All the sights that my eyes will see in Medina

A strange unease remains in my heart O Prophet
Heart will find easiness easy in Medina

How can I tell how my heart's suffered my master
I'll tell my heart's plea to you in Medina

I've heard that Medina's soil sure does heal all
My eyes will line antimony in Medina

I s akin to the floral scent smell of yours
Spread is in my each breath's segment smell of yours

If you do not believe me then ask others
Spreading in all directions went smell of yours

Inside each eye is visible smile of yours
In all the glances did descent smell of yours

For the ones who want to watch your magic charm
See in color changing content smell of yours

Today weather whispered of your arrival
Is it the breeze or a present smell of yours?

A round others make me tongue tied illusion you
should not do
Am reality, making me delusion you should not do

All the human beings that are here are not like the
angels
Revealing your true self out of seclusion you should
not do

Each and every moment is very precious here in this
world
Wasting of the time in such a confusion you should not
do

Heart is fragile thing; it is going to be broken for sure
Overlooking me my dear in exclusion you should not do

It is not a requirement that you do have to like me too
But hiding your youthfulness in seclusion you should not do

Merging of the hearts is not satisfying enough Sabir
Whether one or two of them in conclusion you should not do

N ight went on churning, kept remembering her
Night went on turning, kept remembering her

Time seemed to stop when I looked at the moon
Breaths kept returning, kept remembering her

All night long felt the verve of your besideness
The lamp kept burning, kept remembering her

As time went by, memories kept coming too
Life went on turning, kept remembering her

You were a yearning, and my yearning itself
My yearning kept yearning, remembering her

H er talking style into my being direct went
As if a gust of scent with its strange affect went

Could not see anything else after have now seen you
Cannot figure how to my house I in fact went

After seeing you I lost control of my heart
This too in blames of love, your name as suspect went

Nothing comes into my thoughts except you my dear
Because of you my skill now has all perfect went

After seeing your elegance, now it feels like
Heart's desire to watch the moon with all respect went

Enjoyed both the ends in life by being in love
Sabir lived and died for her, his life's project went

A fter being vocal am perturbed too
Then with some people am bit bothered too

I have kept you in the depths of my heart
Then to have the same treasure desired too

I say not a thing when I do see you
Did you notice that I am cultured too

Lift your gaze but do not put us in awe
Your presence has worshippers acquired too

Ones that look at your beauty, your charm
Discerning of themselves as awkward too

Who is here that does not know how to love
Am not alone, experts have gathered too

All in your presence are not all that well
Some in your love healer have suffered too

W ithout you the heart in unrest can be
With the days bad, the evenings messed can be

How can I leave desert of nuttiness?
Your street in middle of this quest can be

The naive heart just does not understand
So, this way now some heart's lovefest can be

The heart knows very well when to perceive
Even when your thoughts in less quest can be

In good pretense to see her face to face
Good now this meeting in detest can be

It is not just me, others maintaining heart are more
too
In this assembly, the ones with your love's art are more
too

Believe me, people ask of you when they see me
Of course, now due to you my reference chart are more too

I found it crucial to sew my lips for your sake my dear
But then there exist locks on my mind and heart are
more too

There exists fluency in your fervor nevertheless
The modes of beauty you have molded with art are
more too

What is in front of us is not all existence there is,
Searching can lead to suns, moons, in far apart are
more too

From you only is the life's might of mine
From your energy comes the light of mine

After meeting you there is feeling that
Sure, with someone is friendship slight of mine

First the heart fears then it begins to laugh
When it notices despair plight of mine

Be careful walking on frail heart of mine
In it resides the life's twilight of mine

I compose these verses in love of yours
Due to you poetry and write of mine

I just want her to be so beside me
Look Sabir this so simple might of mine

E ven to myself I was so wrong the first time
When a stone in hand I stood along the first time

It must have been written in my fate that someone
Introduced two of us get along the first time

I also like her a lot with all my heart that
It's heart that did tell her real strong the first time

Was it your voice or did you compose melodies?
It seemed that she sang to me a song the first time

Is she fairylike or is she angel being?
I just could not fathom this along the first time

With those magical gazes of hers she for sure
Anointed my heart with a salve strong the first time

A longed desire of mine has been fulfilled today
She did up to my door came along the first time

F riends once more are annoying with ado
With memories employing with ado

Ones that were closer to heart, are now with
Impulsive flashbacks toying with ado

Did my friends return from meeting of foes?
With tests they are deploying with ado!

Now thoughts are only of her, the way she
Dwell in my heart enjoying with ado

Bestow upon me too charity of sight
Your hiding is decoying with ado

It was just matter of her one smile, now
To her Sabir is going with ado

O cean of loves, a strange affair it is
Shore is near but also far where it is

Without being invoked, i am bestowed
All people with such a luck rare it is

Ones those love keep no malice to others
One that loves, to all person fair it is

After inflicting wounds, applies anoint,
Tell me where else such healer there it is

Whether she comes to meet me or does not
Heart remains as always in impair it is

There are so many that like you Sabir
One without friends person despair it is

Song

H ave such a letter I have written
Initiation of ardor I have done
She promises to fulfill fidelity
Spring comes and brings rain
Candle fly is dancing on flowers at night
Nuptial songs are echoing in garden

Goddess of love's anklets are ringing

She is absorbed in her dance

Goddess of faithfulness all stretched in trance

Anklets are singing song of fidelity

How can one now behold one's heart

After losing resolve I am all yours

The whole world delivered to you

And you deliver yourself to me

Love letter is in front of me

From east and west came voices

She is enamored with Sabir

This is the story of our love

O Heart Do Not Tease Me

O heart, do not tease Me
Am afraid that
It may slip out of my tongue
She is not aware
But heart wants
It is a yearning though

That she is face to face with me

Fresh roselike face

On the face a smile

From lips, flowers pouring

Hair as musk

So, the beauty is such that

It is like an unattainable desire

Keep your hopes Sabir

Pray in your heart

That God one day

Brings her in front of you

Desert of Love

I t is the evening of love and beauty
Do not leave me alone world of my life
I do not want to shatter in pieces
This way in all directions
It would only be me and me
Like the desert of love

Your shadow will fall on me
I would be the floor for your feet
Wherever you go in this world
I will be everywhere
Here and there I would be infused in air

May Time Remain in My Hands

What is my place my friend?
Show it to me with your gaze
People around should not know
That would be your favor for me
In your heart is the place for me
But this worry is in my heart

Well, my heart is a different matter

It has no peace nor it is settled

Towards the destination of love my friend

It has it's course with zeal

This journey will not be a waste

Tell me this with your gaze

Do I have to wait for you

People around you should not know

Glance at me with love just once

The time should not slip out of hands this time

Courage for Life

T wo hearts meeting
   In moonlit night
But it still was lost
In all directions in all places
People are just people
Unaware of matters of love

They are thorns that despise flowers

They used to point fingers

Lovers are used to bear hardships

Courage for life

Wait a bit more

In divine realm we know there are delays

But know this,

There is no unfairness

The Story that Used to be

J ust like this at one gathering
I talked to her
The plight of heart too
Was like mine
With broken heart pangs
I was wounded too

The party with her beauty

Was twinkling as if

It was like the fireflies at night

Maybe my words

Were demulcent for her heart

Then she like a fairy

Looked at me with love

Heart was in awe of God's works

It was prostrating

What used to be a story

Has become reality today

Earthquake

L ife until yesterday
Use to dance around in those hills

Fountains of happiness

Were dancing in sways

Naughty kids

Swinging in the arms of breeze

Bells around cattle's neck

Were singing strange songs

Youth's faces full of hopes

Were planting dreams in the eyes

Aged faces

Under shadows of peace

Immersed in their pasts

But one shifting from the ground

Desolated all those dreams

Relieved many bodies of their lives

Ones who survived

In the cold weather

Stares at the skies

People of the world

Are asleep in apathy

Now God in human form will have to help humans

But Have Left the Heart There

Your charisma was on display all night
There was a lot of talk of your beauty
The veil kept moving from the face
That is so moonlike
Some said you're a heavenly nymph
I said that it is divine light

Each person said what they could

All were in love with you

Sabir too was devoted to you

Then the time arrived

I left towards home

Without the heart

That I left somewhere, not sure where

You might know perhaps

So easy seems going away of yours
Admiring excuses array of yours

Go wherever you think you need to go
With you the devotee will stay of yours

She just does not let me be at all, now
Am remembering torture play of yours

That so youth-like beauty that is of yours,
But then, hiding the face portray of yours

I do remember that at my questions
Lifting of that low gaze that way of yours

All my teasing of you like that my dear
And then the scarf twirling sway of yours

You do not worry about others now
Since I am yours all is at bay of yours

S pring has returned let the vase be decorated
Then on vase butterfly to be situated

Birds are twittering and chirping among flowers
My beloved also today be invited

The smiling flowers are a source of strength for me
Memories' wilderness can now be visited

Has been ages since I put bracelet on her arm
Now in thoughts that bracelet should be circulated

Ones lost during day do return at the evening
Hopes like these in the hearts should be decorated

One of these days it will grow into a thick tree
Seed of patience in the heart has to be planted

P eople what they say do not do
  Then what I ask they do not do

Such is uncertainty in love
Plan to say but say do not do

Have raised hands to pray for you, so,
When you go away do not do

Though opened window to my house
Open heart's doorway do not do

The ones that kept scents forever
The new wreath array do not do

It's good to live in heart Sabir
Lift hand from heart nay do not do

W hatever it is that occurred, could not forget you
After many torments endured, could not forget you

I could not understand the meaning of loyalties
With this one question I adjured, could not forget you

You broke the promise about being a companion
Despite all anguishes absurd, could not forget you

Your modesty required me to stay away for you
Though this one thought was so preferred, could not
forget you

Whatever your tongue kept saying my heart accepted
With this odd condition occurred, could not forget you

Unusual ups and downs were on the path Sabir
But faced with the declines conferred, could not forget
you

Nothing else is now my aim darling
Now on my lips is your name darling

Do take away your hand from others
Wish with me few steps you came darling

If this is start of monikers then,
Then think what the end will claim darling

Sit, bit more beside me this evening
May not rekindle this flame darling

Your speech is so strange, but consider
Sabir's this composed exclaim darling

U pon evenings' arrival missing you agonizes me
The silent audibles that could be your voice so
rhapsodizes me

The thoughts do sure distract me for a bit during my
daily tasks
Then the memories that keep on coming is what
exercises me

What can I say, I surmise it as if it is so very true
That you're now surely beside me the reverie devises me

In the lines of my both hands is so well written your
name my dear
Though countless times the scheme of things erases
and despises me

I have decorated my heart with only her picture Sabir
The picture of hers is very appealing and apprises me

B reaking of heart is what gain to you
What will this act seek in vain to you

A heart is more fragile than a glass
What bits pieces will attain to you

Love sure is a very cruel thing
Folks scattered here there mundane to you

Hearts do get a lot closer through love
Or else distance will remain to you

Gatherings have people in them, but,
Not single console of pain to you

First, go and learn the meaning of love
Then God will be an attain to you

A Mother's Woe on School Massacre

What lightening fell
All flowers burned
Is this my life or is it a world of mourning?
In my lap, there is sorrow of death
He had just left smiling
Then after that

Air had his blood in it

Who were those people?

Filled me with fire

And stole the resolve from my heart and eyes

It is said, they take lives in name of religion

What sort of religions are they followers of?

To me, barbarians have no religion

God will give me endurance but,

They will not have a moment of solace

They will wander in their own prisons

They will never get a moment of escape

Y ou can keep saying that it can told be not
  Though what is in the heart can withhold be not

Eventually that day too will arrive
What is to be will be and control be not

People do have the keenness to be in love
But bearing its burdens they behold be not

The matters of the heart do become well known
Though even to myself can it told be not

A meeting or separation, what was it?
That unknown happened that night can told be not

Spent the entire life on trust of a promise
What was said in that pledge though can told be not

There used to exist fondness between us once
Possible to forget that thing old be not

Eternal is that life that is full of love
Any furthermore it be controlled be not

So very much vast hearted is this Sabir
This one matter by you can withhold be not

F lowers are what make the gardens decorated
With garden is what I sure am fascinated

I always meet people with a smile on my face
This sure is good habit I have generated

Speaking with the people in charming softer tones
At times it sure does turn out to be ill fated

There may not be any enmity there but still
I admit that yes am a bit aggravated

Jasmines sapling is so very appealing
Can I sit by you, can it be tolerated?

Some friends are going to visit me this evening
You come too, an invite for you too is slated

Whether occasion of happiness or sorrow
Some odd luck the flowers do have for them fated

Your hair is playing with the breeze with such a flair
Is with the air that your hair infatuated?

Whether it happens to be your face or a flower
With both of them my heart's comfort is created

M atters do not cease and keep coming in arrays
Problems do keep on increasing in all their ways

Joy is tied secure with the thread of suffering
Mutual relations do not easily faze

Even when life may seem to be a bit prolonged
But for the sake of love there are not enough days

Both for sure have been made for each other alone
Exact same happen to be beauty and love's ways

Seeking comes with the same measure of its own lack
The distance can increase in the opposite ways

I have been carrying love affair with my pen
Affairs like these that are certain my getaways

There is well being in walking with a head bowed
It just takes a moment for life to end and faze

No one merrily dresses and lies in coffin
When the time to go comes Sabir, no one then stays

Diana Krall

A better singer than you are there no one here
Achieved the styles of your lofty flair no one here

Several waves of sounds can arise in the heart
To the splendor of yours can compare no one here

I stand so tall when admiring your craftiness
Receives such immense praise to compare no one here

Though there are other crooners around in the world
But a songster such as you are there no one here

Your musicians have unique composing skills
Vocalizing the words like your air no one here

Many artists are analyzed by gatherings
Like your heart alluring voice's flair no one here

Many around here declare their singing skills
But a second like you can compare no one here

No Heart is Empty of Love in the World

Y ou are looking for fate
Let me tell you something
What is written is destined
Is in front of the eyes
Each evening brings
Airs of love

Fluttering of the scarf

Makes hair dance in the air

Face shimmering

Red henna of hands

Is so appealing

Eyes with black eyeliner

And the long hair

On face the smile

Or is it perfume in air

Redness of the lips

And then in red dress

Necklace of pearls

Is so accurate around the neck

With suddenness has arrived

Your fullness over puberty

In between flowers then

Pause by you

This evening is heartfelt

Lovely sight has appeared

I have brought a flower

To sew on garment

Golden twinkles

Favorite bracelets

Is a simple gift

It is for you alone

Go ahead wear them

Enhance the beauty

It will be like the moon

Then this form of yours

This vivacity of mine

Live for ever

Live forever like this

Our love too

Till this world lasts

Will be discussing of us

In townships and dwellings

Will sing song of love

It is due to the love

The whole world exists

Not empty of love

Song

C louds thunder rain drops
   Rainy season brought the floral spring
Birds singing, cuckoo cooing
Peacocks dancing in the courtyard
How nice is your adornment
Goddess of love worships love

Pretty one dances at the drum beat

Jingle clink singing anklets

Hair locks waving like serpent

Around the neck shines necklace of candle fly

Each hair strand with stars and moons

Earrings made of pearls

Fragile body elastic body

Shot an arrow from eyes that

Wounded my heart

Your songs are melodious O queen

Erotic redness on lips

With many folds frantic happiness

Around neck peaceful garland

Give Sabir peacefulness

Live Forever Ruler of Heart

Wet dress
    Eye-lines
On face Wine drops twinkling
Monsoon brought dark clouds
Rain in courtyard drizzle
On arms bracelets of all colors

Reddish dress

Black apparel

Shoes are golden

What sight you have displayed lady

Someone tipsy is deliberating stories

Causing anxieties in minds

This is the tradition of love, beloved

Goddess of love adores Sabir wrote love story

Be forever ruler of heart

Kashmir

T his one night shall pass too people of Kashmir
Morning will come anew people of Kashmir

The Valley of Kashmir is all your domain
One day regained by you people of Kashmir

Kashmir is yours and it will be remain yours
Chains will sing this song true people of Kashmir

The separated ones will unite again,
That feast will come to you people of Kashmir

Sabir is praying to God to be with you
Your haven be in view people of Kashmir

Sculptor

L ook how he casts the statues
The one that endowed you this talent
In shapes of Gods and Goddesses
You carve visages of that one
Yes, but you should know this
He makes bodies out of dust

Then upon his beckoning
Blood starts running in the dust
The entire lives that those figures
Sculpt themselves

I agree that you are an artist
An artist from whose hands
Stones get the beauty such
It creates longing in heart

But remember this much
The one that resides in skies
Is the best of sculptors
You do not have his talents
His art does not decline

An already burnt heart you are burning why
In love and affection all this spurning why

If the fate has all these tests written in it
Then bring together two hearts concerning why

If delights are mere for few years of this life
Lord of the seasons all this sojourning why

Neither complaint to someone nor a protest
Then tell the worlds' merry laughter turning why

After promising lifelong of perseverance
You then just left me without returning why

Each wound now has blood oozing from it Sabir
Faithfulness to be forgetting spurning why

To the heart, radiant dream adorning is good
Those dreams to be hidden, uniforming is good

The dreams and thoughts just have only your images
Dreaming of you in such a weaved forming is good

How can it be told that heart has no clear moments
When you don't come, your excuse informing is good

In the lonely nights, it's you and your reflection
Across the moon, your face's alluring is good

There are hymns and praises upon your arrival
Melodic singing of birds in morning is good

In heart's garden Sabir, reside her memories
With her memories, blooms of flowering is good

Books by Andaaz Publication

Available on www.amazon.com
or
www.andaazpublications.com

انداز پبلیکیشنز کی دیگر مطبوعات

ذرا موسم بدلنے دو	سلیم کوثر
دنیا مری آرزو سے کم ہے	سلیم کوثر
محبت اک شجر ہے	سلیم کوثر
یہ چراغ ہے تو جلا رہے	سلیم کوثر
خالی ہاتھوں میں ارض و سما	سلیم کوثر
میں نے اسمِ محمد صلی اللہ علیہ وسلم کو لکھا بہت	سلیم کوثر
اندوختہ	انور شعور
می رقصم	انور شعور
مشقِ سخن	انور شعور
دل کا کیا رنگ کروں	انور شعور
ڈاؤنامہ	ڈاکٹر حبیب خان
مجتبیٰ حسین اور فنِ طنز و مزاح نگاری	ڈاکٹر گل راعنا
صدائے سخن	خواجہ وہاب صابرؔ
ابھی ہم تمہارے ہیں	الماس شبی
کچھ خواب اُٹھائے پھرتا ہوں	فیاض الدین صائب

available on www.amazon.com

OR

www.andaazpublications.com

www.ingramcontent.com/pod-product-compliance
Lightning Source LLC
Chambersburg PA
CBHW060031050426
42448CB00012B/2954